Cats are Fun!

Written by
Jill Atkins

Ransom

Cats are so soft.

Can you see sharp teeth,
pointed ears and a long tail?

Cats can get up to all sorts of antics.

They might go up a ladder or sip from the tap.

Kittens are fun too.

This kitten is having so much fun!

This kitten is sitting in the sink

... and this kitten is sitting in a box.

Is that kitten sitting in a pot?

I think it must be fond of that pot!

But how did that cat get so high up on that shelf?

Did it jump?

How will it get down?

This cat might go
in the garden in the sun,
but not if it is raining.

If the sun is hot, a cat might rest on a garden bench or sit on a deck chair.

It looks as if this cat has been hunting.

I think it got a rat!

Yuck!

This cat is hunting for fish in a pond.

I think it just might get a fish.

Is this cat going to pinch
a fish at the market?

This cat is high up on a roof.

This cat is up on a roof, too.
But now it is dark and the moon is up.

Will the cat yowl in the night
and disturb you?

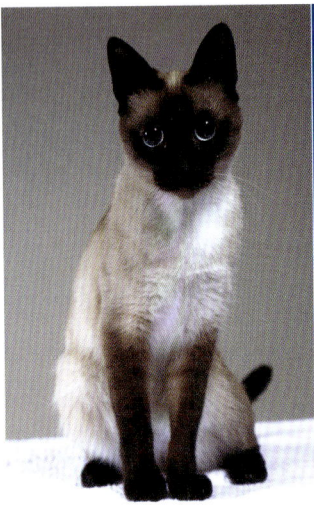

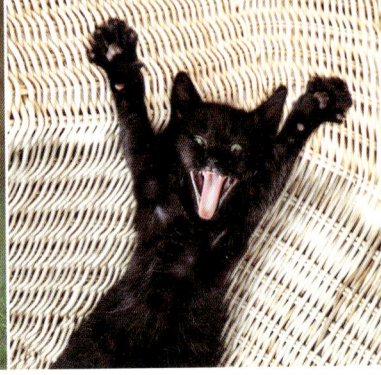

Look at all the cats.

Cats **must** be the best pets!